Song

The library i
It's got a lot ings to do and see!
The library is for you and me!

The library has got a gallery,
It's got a multimedia room, too!
Let's go to the library! It's new!
Chorus

The library has got a reading corner,
It's got an information desk, too!
Let's go to the library! It's new!
Chorus

Lesson 2

1. (0.06) Read and sing.
2. (0.08) Listen and answer. *True* or *false*?
3. Make sentences about the picture.

Grammar

The library **has got** a gallery.
The library **hasn't got** a bedroom.

I can shine!

4. Talk about your school library.

The library hasn't got a gallery.

The library has got an information desk.

I can say what the library has and hasn't got.

1 0.09 Listen, point and say.

1
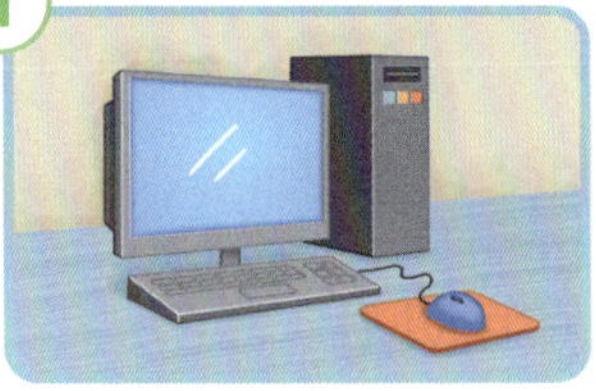
computer

2

poster

3

television

4

beanbag

2 0.10 Listen or watch. What do the children find in the courtyard?

3 Read again. Then answer. *True* or *false*?

1 The reading corner has got posters.
2 The library has got a monster.
3 Biscuit is in the multimedia room.

I can shine!

4 Act out the story.

I can read, understand and act out a story about a library.

Lesson 4

1 0.11 Listen and count. Then say the missing numbers.

2 Play the game.

3 0.12 Listen and read. Then chant.

Grammar builder

Has the reading corner got	*books?*	*Yes, it has.*
Has the multimedia room got	*books?*	*No, it hasn't.*

I can shine!

4 Ask and answer.

Has the multimedia room got computers?

Yes, it has.

Has your classroom got a television?

No, it hasn't.

I can say what things places have got.

Lesson 5

1 0.14 Listen and number. Then ask and answer.

a

b

c

d

What time is it?

It's one o'clock / half past one.

2 0.15 Say the activities they can do. Then listen and check.

Library Activity Day!

Wednesday 9–4.30

9.00	9.30	10.30	12.00	1.30	3.00
Welcome!	**Painting** Learn to paint animals.	**Film club** Watch an adventure film.	**Lunchtime!** Pizza, salad and sandwiches.	**Computer club** Play computer games with your friends.	**Story time** Listen to your favourite books.

1

What time is it?

It's half past nine.

2

What time is it?

It's three o'clock.

Which activity at the library do you want to do?

I can shine!

3 Tell a friend about an activity you do.

What activity do you do?

I go to football club on Monday.

What time is football club?

I can talk about the time of activities.

Our library records

Step 1 Review

1 Describe the pictures. Then ask and answer.

It's a reading corner. It's got... .

Has it got...?

Step 2 Create

2 Draw a cover for your library record.

3 Ask and answer.

This is the reading corner.

Has the reading corner got books?

Yes, it has.

Time to shine!

4 Present your library record to the class.

This is my library record.

I can talk about a library.

1 All about school!

Rise and Shine Library

- Say what I've got at school each day.
- Read about subjects and daily routines.
- Say how I go to school.
- Write a diary entry.
- Create a photo diary.

1 Maths	2 ICT	3 Science	4 History	5 PE
6 Drama	7 Geography	8 English	9 Art	10 Music

Lesson 1

I like Art. What subject do you like?

What can you see?

1 1.01 **Listen and find.**

2 1.02 **Listen and point. Then listen and repeat.**

3 **Watch and listen.**

4 1.03 **Listen and say. Then play the game.**

I wonder...
Are school days the same in every country?

Song

Every day I go to school,
School is fun! School is cool!

What have you got on Monday?
On Monday at school?
I've got Maths and Geography!
How about you?
Chorus
What have you got on Tuesday?
On Tuesday at school?
I've got Art and Music!
How about you?
Chorus
What have you got on Wednesday?
On Wednesday at school?
I've got Science and PE. How about you?
Chorus

	Daniel	Rafa	Alicia	Lena
Monday	Art	PE	ICT	History

Lesson 2

1. 1.04 Read and sing.
2. 1.06 Listen and answer. *True* or *false*?
3. What have you got on Monday? Say.

Grammar

What have you got on Monday?
I've got Art and Geography on Monday.

I can shine!

4. Ask and answer.

What have you got on Tuesday?

I've got... .

I can say what I've got at school each day.

Lesson 3

1 1.08 Listen, point and say.

1

wake up

2

brush my teeth

3

have breakfast

4

have a shower

5

go to school

6

go to bed

2 Look at the story. What subjects can you see?

3 1.09 Listen or watch. What do you learn about teeth?

4 Read again. Then match.

1 Alicia
2 Daniel
3 Rafa
4 Lena

a I've only got 19 teeth.
b I go to bed at eight o'clock.
c Maths can be fun!
d I think I like Maths now.

I can shine!

5 Imagine you are Daniel at the school subject fair. Act out.

I can read, understand and act out a story about subjects and routines.

Story value Understanding the importance of all subjects.

Lesson 4

1 1.10 Listen. Which timeline shows Lena's day?

A

B

2 1.11 Listen and read. Then chant.

Grammar builder

What time do you	wake up?	I wake up at half past six.
	brush your teeth?	I brush my teeth at seven o'clock.

3 Ask and answer for you.

What time do you wake up?

I wake up at half past seven.

Structures *What time do you (wake up)? I wake up at (seven o'clock).*

Lesson 5

1 Look. What transport can you see?

2 1.12 Listen and read. Then answer for Anna.

by bus | walk | by bike | by car

3 1.13 Listen again and repeat.

Pronunciation

4 1.14 Listen and say.

The boys walk to school.
They take their toys and they talk.

I can shine!

5 Ask and answer. Find out how your friends go to school.

How do you go to school?

I go to school by car.

I can say how I go to school.

Global Citizen

I appreciate different school days.

Lesson 6

1 Look. Is your school day different?

2 (1.15) Listen and read. What subjects has Chen got on Monday morning?

Hi! I'm Chen and I'm from China. This is a **timetable** for my school day.

TIME	MONDAY
7.30	Maths
8.30	English
9.30	History
10.30	Break
11.30	Geography
12.30	Lunch
2.30	Art
3.30	ICT
4.30	Music

I wake up at half past six. I go to school by bus at seven o'clock.

This is my **classroom**. Classes start at half past seven. There are 40 students in my class! On Monday, we've got Maths, English, History and Geography in the morning.

We have lunch and we play in the **playground**. We have two hours!

I go home at five o'clock. I do **homework**. I go to bed at half past nine. I'm tired!

3 Read again. Then answer for Chen. *True* or *false*?

1 My timetable tells me what subjects I've got.
2 There are 40 students in my class.
3 We have classes in the playground.
4 I haven't got homework.

Do you like every day at school? Why or why not?

4 (1.16) Listen. What's Chen's favourite day?

Lesson 7

1 1.18 Listen and read. What's Carla's favourite day?

My favourite day is Thursday. I have breakfast at school. I've got Science, Maths, Art and English. I help in my school library on Thursday afternoon. It's fun!

Carla

Our writing workshop

2 1.19 **Ideas generator** Read, listen and complete.

1

My favourite day is Tuesday. I've got... .

2

My favourite day is Friday. I go to school by... .

3 **Give it a go** Plan your diary entry with a friend.

Choose your favourite day at school.

What subjects have you got?

What other things do you do?

I can shine!

4 Write your diary entry together.

I can write a diary entry.

My school day photo diary

Step 1 Review

1 Write the words.

brush my teeth wake up Wednesday
Geography Maths Friday Science have a shower
Monday go to bed ICT History

School days	School subjects	Things I do every day

2 What do you do before you go to school?

3 Ask and answer about your school day.

What time do you wake up?

I wake up at half past seven.

How do you go to school?

I walk to school.

4 Read and complete.

timetable homework classroom playground

1 At lunchtime, I play in the… .
2 After school, I do my… .
3 My school subjects are on my… .
4 I have lessons in the… .

5 Watch and listen.

Step 2 Create

6 Choose your favourite school day.

7 Tell your group about your favourite day. Take photos or draw the things you do on that day together.

I like Wednesday.

What have we got on Wednesday?

We've got English, Maths, Science and Art.

8 Create a photo diary.

Time to shine!

9 Present your photo diary to the class.

10 What's your favourite school day?

I wake up at half past six. I have breakfast at seven o'clock.

We've got Geography, PE and History on Thursday.

I can talk about my school days.

2 Explore our town!

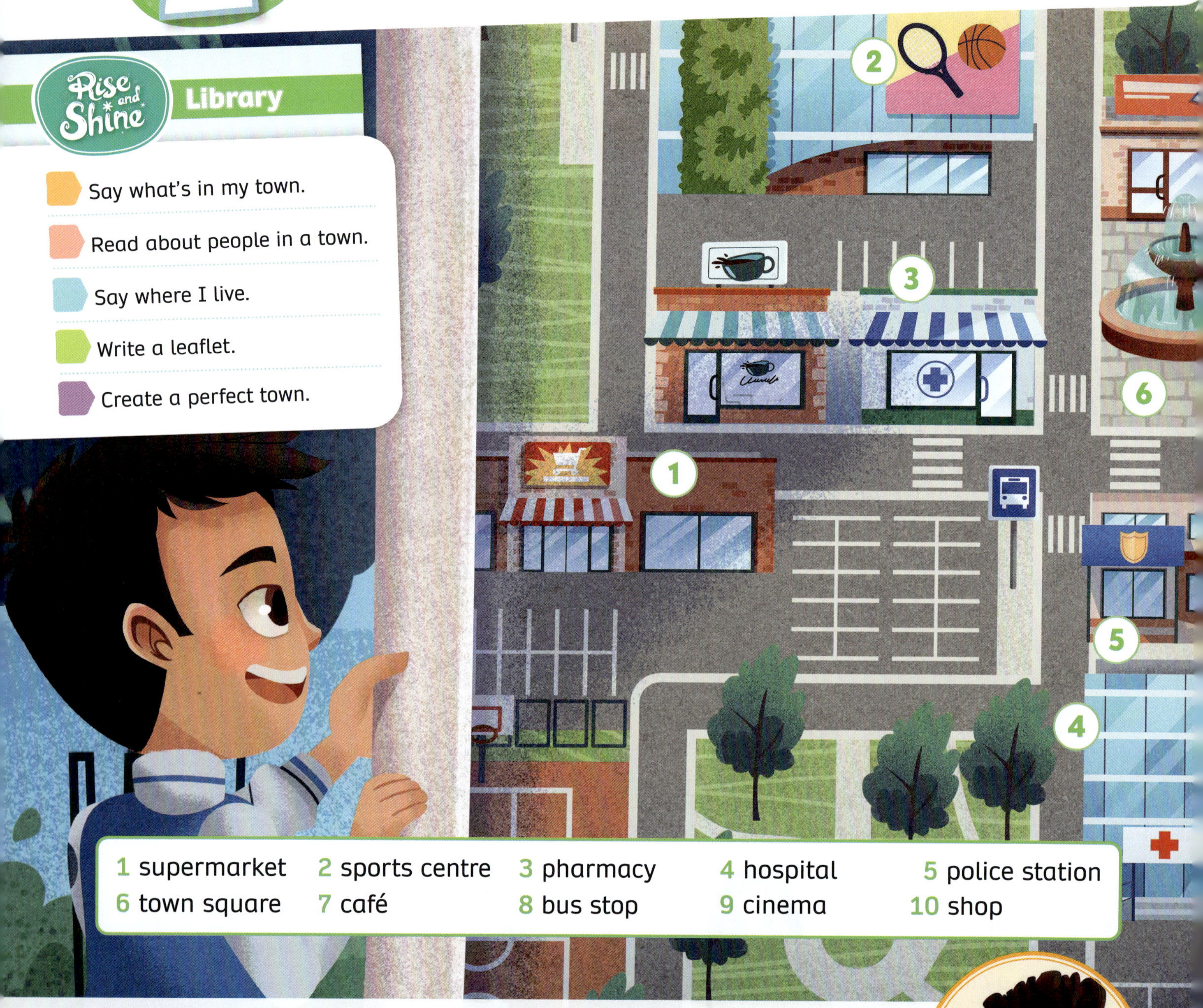

Rise and Shine Library

- Say what's in my town.
- Read about people in a town.
- Say where I live.
- Write a leaflet.
- Create a perfect town.

1 supermarket	2 sports centre	3 pharmacy	4 hospital	5 police station
6 town square	7 café	8 bus stop	9 cinema	10 shop

Lesson 1

I go to the cinema. Where do you go in your town?

What can you see?

1 2.01 **Listen and find.**

2 2.02 **Listen and point. Then listen and repeat.**

3 **Watch and listen.**

4 **Ask and answer.**

What's this?

It's a café.

Song

This is my town,
Come with me!
There are a lot of places,
Come and see!

There's a town square, there's a café.
There's a sports centre – I go on Sunday!

Chorus

There are supermarkets and some shops.
There are buses and some bus stops.

Chorus

There aren't any hospitals, there isn't a cinema.
But there's a police station with a police car.

Chorus

I wonder...
What can you do in a town square?

Lesson 2

1 2.03 Read and sing.

2 2.05 Listen and answer. *True* or *false*?

3 Make sentences about the picture.

Grammar

There are some shops.
There aren't any schools.

I can shine!

4 Talk about your town.

In my town, there are some... .

There aren't any... .

I can say what's in my town.

Lesson 3

1 2.07 Listen, point and say.

1

doctor

2

shop assistant

3

librarian

4

bus driver

5

waiter

6

police officer

2 Look at the story. What jobs can you see?

3 2.08 Listen or watch. What do the children find?

Rise and Shine — Library

4 Read again. Then answer.

1. Where do the children find the book?
2. Who do the children ask for help?
3. What do they find in the book?
4. Where do they see the doctor?

I can shine!

5 Imagine you find the doctor's book. Act out.

I can read, understand and act out a story about people in a town.

Lesson 4

1 2.09 Listen. Who's in the town square?

2 2.10 Listen and read. Then chant.

Ask and answer about the town square.

Grammar builder

Is there a	*librarian?*	*Yes, there is.*
	bus driver?	*No, there isn't.*
Are there any	*police officers?*	*Yes, there are.*
	teachers?	*No, there aren't.*

3 Ask and answer for you.

Is there a pharmacy in your town?

Yes, there is.

Lesson 5

1 Look. What places can you see?

2 2.11 Listen and read. Then answer for Nathan.

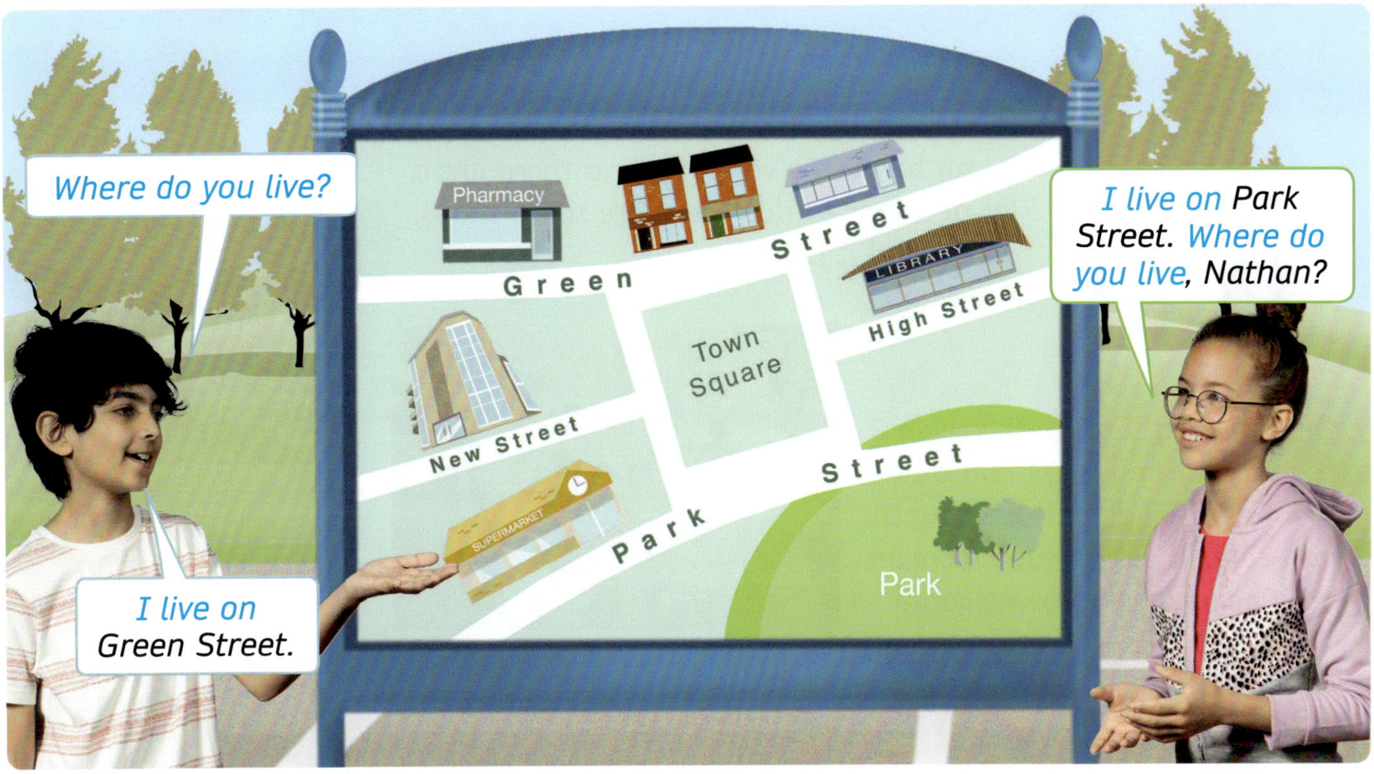

3 2.12 Listen again and repeat.

Pronunciation time

4 2.13 Listen and say.

I can shine!

5 Ask and answer. Find out where your friends live.

Where do you live?

I live... .

I can say where I live.

Global Citizen

I learn about different towns.

Lesson 6

1 Look. What can you see in the town square?

2 2.14 Listen and read. What can you do in the town square?

Hi! I'm Molly. This is the Old Market Square in my town. It's very big, and there are a lot of things to do. There are some shops, a café and a **fountain**.

On Saturday, I go to the town square with my mum and dad. We meet friends and have lunch in a café. Then we eat ice cream on a **bench** in the town square.

In the summer, there's a beach in the town square! It's great! The children play and their mums and dads sit and talk. There aren't any cars, but there are a lot of people. I love my town and my **community**. People here are very **friendly**.

3 Read again. Choose the correct word to complete each sentence.

1 The town square is... .
2 There's a... .
3 There aren't any... .
4 Every year, there's a... .
5 People in the town are very... .

beach
fountain
cars
friendly
big

Where do people meet in your town?

4 2.15 Listen. What people are there in Molly's town?

Lesson 7

1 2.17 Listen and read. What's Alvaro's favourite place?

My Town

There's a town square. It's got a nice café. There isn't a cinema.

There are some fountains. They're fun!

My favourite place is the library. The librarian helps me.

Our writing workshop

2 2.18 **Ideas generator** Listen, read and match.

1

Lydia

a There's a bus stop in my town centre. The bus driver helps me.

2

Carlos

b There's a bookshop. The shop assistant helps me to find books.

3 **Give it a go** Plan your leaflet with a friend.

What places are there in your town?

What places aren't there in your town?

Who helps you in your town?

I can shine!

4 Write your leaflet together.

I can write a leaflet.

My perfect town

Step 1 Review

1 Write the words.

librarian doctor bus stop hospital supermarket
pharmacy café shop assistant police station bus driver
sports centre waiter police officer library

Places	People

2 Where can you see the people in Activity 1? Say.

There's a librarian in the library.

3 Name the places on the map. Then ask and answer.

Is there a café?

Yes, there is.

Where do you live?

I live on… .

4 Tell a friend about your favourite place in town.

1 Where is it?
2 What people are there?
3 How do they help you?

My favourite place in town is the sports centre. My swimming teacher helps me.

5 Watch and listen.

Step 2 Create

6 Choose the places and people in your perfect town.

7 Tell your group about your people and places.

Is there a hospital?

Yes, there is. There are some doctors, too.

8 Create a map of your perfect town.

Time to shine!

9 Present your town map to the class.

10 Which is your favourite town map?

I can talk about my town and community.

Review 1 All about us

1 (2.20) Listen. What subjects have Cameron and Zora got today?

2 Look. Ask and answer.

café | theatre | school | bus driver | waiters | teachers | doctors

Is there a… ?

Are there any… ?

3 Think about people in your school and town. Who helps you?

4 (2.21) Listen and read. Is it Cameron's or Zora's diary?

Monday

On Monday, I wake up at seven o'clock. I have breakfast and I brush my teeth. Then I go to school by bus. There's a bus stop on my street. Monday is my favourite day. I've got PE, Maths and Music. After school, I go to the sports centre with my friends. In the evening, I do my homework. I go to bed at half past nine.

5 Read again. Then answer about the diary. *True* or *false*?

1. I wake up at 7.00.
2. I walk to school.
3. I like PE and Maths.
4. There isn't a bus stop on my street.
5. I go to bed at 9.30.

MINI PROJECT

6 Write your diary for Monday.

On Monday, I wake up ... .
I go to school by... .
I've got... .
After school, I... .

Time to shine!

7 What can you see in the courtyard? Complete your library record.

1	I can read, write and say school subjects and places in a town.
2	I can ask and answer about routines and people in my town.
3	I can say how I go to school.
4	I can ask friends where they live.

3 Let's tell stories!

Rise and Shine Library

- Talk about book characters.
- Read about book characters.
- Agree and disagree.
- Write a book review.
- Create story characters.

I wonder...
What other ways can we tell stories?

1 giant	2 astronaut	3 prince	4 princess	5 spy
6 storyteller	7 pirate	8 monster	9 superhero	10 dragon

Lesson 1

What characters are there in your favourite books?

What can you see?

1 3.01 **Listen and find.**

2 3.02 **Listen and point. Then listen and repeat.**

3 **Watch and listen.**

4 **Ask and answer.**

Who's this?

A superhero.

Song

Storyteller, storyteller!
What's the book about?
Let's open it and see!

The book is about a giant.
Is she happy or is she sad?
Is she good or is she bad?
Please read it to me!
Yes, of course!

Chorus

The book is about a dragon.
Is it short or is it tall?
Is it big or is it small?
Please read it to me!
Yes, of course!

Chorus

Lesson 2

1 Read and sing. (3.03)

2 Listen, find and point. (3.05)

3 Make a sentence, a question and an answer about a book in the picture.

Grammar

The book is about a giant.
Is she happy? Yes, she is. No, she isn't.

I can shine!

4 Ask and answer.

The book is about a princess.

Is she happy?

No, she isn't.

I can talk about book characters.

Lesson 3

1 3.07 Listen, point and say.

1

cute

2

scary

3

clever

4

brave

5

kind

6

strong

2 Look at the story. Describe the book characters you can see.

3 3.08 Listen or watch. Who likes the book about spies?

4 Read again. Describe the book characters.

I can shine!

5 Imagine you are showing your friends your favourite books. Act out.

I can read, understand and act out a story about book characters.

Lesson 4

1 3.09 Listen. What's Oscar's favourite book?

2 3.10 Listen and read. Then chant.

Grammar builder

Are the dragons	*clever?*	*Yes, they are.*
Are they	*scary?*	*No, they aren't.*

3 Ask and answer.

Are the cats cute?

Yes, they are.

Structures *Are they (clever)? Yes, they are. / No, they aren't.*

Lesson 5

1 Look. What story characters can you see?

2 3.11 Listen and read. Which book do they both like?

3 3.12 Listen again and repeat.

Pronunciation

4 3.13 Listen and say.

The book is about a very clever robot and a very brave boy!

I can shine!

5 Find out what your friends think of different books. Agree and disagree.

I like The amazing astronaut.

So do I!

I can agree and disagree.

Lesson 6

1 Look. How can we tell stories?

2 3.14 Listen and read. What types of storytelling use dance?

Opera

Opera tells **interesting** stories with songs. Opera is from Italy. The stories are about princesses and pirates. They're also about normal people and families.

Hula

This is Hula. It's from Hawaii. The dance and the chant tell stories about people and the past. It's **fun** to watch. Dancers wear skirts and flowers. Children can learn Hula in special schools in Hawaii.

Kathak Dance

Look at the dancers. They're telling stories with dance. The name of the dance is 'Kathak'. It's from India. The stories are about princes and princesses. The dancers wear very **beautiful** clothes!

Chinese Shadow Puppets

These are Chinese shadow puppets. The puppets tell a story. The stories are about princesses, brave explorers and scary dragons. There's a lot of action and it's very **exciting**!

3 Read again. Then answer.

Which type of storytelling...

1 has a lot of things happening and is exciting?
2 isn't from Hawaii and is a dance?
3 is interesting and tells stories with songs?
4 is fun to see and the dancers wear flowers?

Which type of storytelling do you like? Why?

4 3.15 Listen. Which type of storytelling do they do?

Lesson 7

1 3.17 Listen and read. Is it a good book review?

Poppy and Polly Save the World

★★★★★

I like the book. It's about a spy and a pirate. They're clever and brave. There's a giant in the story. He's scary. The story is very exciting.

Our writing workshop

2 3.18 **Ideas generator** Listen, read and complete.

1
My book is about… .
They're strong and clever.

2
My book is interesting.
It's about superheroes.
They're… and kind.

3 **Give it a go** Plan your review with a friend.

The book is about… .
They are… .
The story is… .

I can shine!

4 Write your book review together.

I can write a book review.

Our story characters

Step 1 Review

1 Look and match.

dragons | spies | superheroes | giants | prince and princess | astronauts

a 

b 

c 

d 

e 

f 

2 Describe the characters in Activity 1.

brave | strong | cute | clever | kind | scary

3 Ask and answer about the books.

The book is about dragons.

Are they cute?

Yes, they are.

4 Tell a friend about your favourite book.

1 The book is about… .
2 The characters are… .
3 I think the book is… .

My favourite book is about a pirate. He's strong. I think the book is interesting.

5 Watch and listen.

Step 2 Create

6 Choose your story character.

7 Tell your group about your character.

My story character is a dragon. He's clever.

I like dragons.

So do I.

8 Create your story characters.

Time to shine!

9 Present your characters to the class.

10 Tell stories together!

It's a dragon.

It's a spy.

I can talk about story characters.

4 Party at the library!

Rise and Shine **Library**

- Say what people like and don't like doing.
- Read about a party.
- Say what I'm good at.
- Write instructions.
- Create a new hobby.

I wonder... What hobbies use paper?

1 playing computer games 2 juggling 3 taking photos 4 learning an instrument
5 acting 6 coding 7 having a party 8 painting
9 playing chess 10 swapping cards

My favourite hobby is painting. What's your favourite hobby?

Lesson 1

What can you see?

1 4.01 **Listen and find.**

2 4.02 **Listen and point. Then listen and repeat.**

3 **Watch and listen.**

4 **Ask and answer.**

What do you like doing?

I like playing chess.

	☺	☹
Lena	taking photos	acting
Rafa	juggling	playing video games
Daniel	painting	coding
Alicia	learning an instrument	swapping cards

Song

There's a party at the library,
We're all having fun.
There are a lot of different hobbies,
There's a hobby for everyone!

He likes painting pictures,
She likes acting.
He doesn't like playing chess,
But I think it's amazing!
Chorus

She likes learning an instrument,
He likes juggling,
She doesn't like taking photos,
But I like doing everything!
Chorus

Lesson 2

1. 4.03 Read and sing.
2. 4.05 Listen, find and say. Who is it?
3. Make sentences about Rafa.

Grammar

She likes taking photos.
He doesn't like playing chess.

I can shine!

4. Ask and answer. Then say.

Do you like acting?
Yes, I do.
Sara likes acting.

I can talk about what people like and don't like doing.

Lesson 3

1 4.07 Listen, point and say.

1

doing crafts

2

being outside

3

using computers

4

helping people

5

learning something new

6

doing sport

2 Look at the story. Find the activities from Activity 1.

3 4.08 Listen or watch. Who learns a new hobby?

Rise and Shine

Library

4 Read again. Then answer. *True* or *false*?

1 Lena and Rafa are in the multimedia room.
2 Rafa wants to learn to juggle.
3 Lena likes helping people.
4 The children decorate the reading corner.

I can shine!

5 Imagine you are at the party. Act out.

I can read, understand and act out a story about a party.

Lesson 4

1 Listen and match. (4.09)

Alicia | Lena | Daniel | Rafa

2 Listen and read. Then chant. (4.10)

Grammar builder

Does she like	*doing sport?*	*Yes, she does.*
Does he like	*being outside?*	*No, he doesn't.*

Ask and answer about Thomas.

3 Ask and answer about a friend.

Does Marco like helping people?

Yes, he does.

Structures *Does he / she like (being outside)? Yes, he / she does. / No, he / she doesn't.*

Lesson 5

1 Look. What hobbies can you see?

2 4.11 Listen and read. What's Shaun good at?

3 4.12 Listen again and repeat.

Pronunciation

4 4.13 Listen and say.

This girl likes learning new things.
She's good at singing and dancing.
She's amazing!

I can shine!

5 Ask and answer. Find out what your friends are good at.

Are you good at doing crafts?

Yes, I am.

I can say what I'm good at and what I want to learn.

Lesson 6

1 Look. What type of activities are they?

2 4.14 Listen and read. What crafts use paper?

Fun hobbies

Origami

I like doing crafts. My favourite craft is origami. The Japanese word *origami* means to **fold** paper. I like making animals. I'm very good at making frogs and birds. My sister likes origami, too. She's good at making flowers. She isn't very good at making animals but she likes learning and I like helping her!

Scrapbooking

I like making scrapbooks. I find and **cut** photos to **stick** in my scrapbooks. I'm very good at taking photos. I like taking photos and painting pictures for my scrapbooks too. I've got a lot of different scrapbooks. I've got a scrapbook about being outside and a scrapbook about doing sports.

Finger knitting

Finger knitting is a great craft. You use your fingers to **knit** with wool. I like using a lot of different colours. I'm very good at making beautiful scarves for my dolls and teddies.

3 Read again. Then say the hobby.

1 You knit with wool.
2 You fold paper.
3 You cut and stick pictures.
4 You can make animals and flowers.
5 You can make scarves and clothes.

What hobby can you teach a friend?

4 4.15 Listen. What's the hobby?

Lesson 7

1 4.17 Listen and read. What animal does the girl make?

Making a paper animal

1 Cut out the paper.

2 Fold green and yellow paper.

3 Stick on the head and the eyes.

Our writing workshop

2 4.18 **Ideas generator** Listen, read and match.

1 Making a scrapbook

2 Making a birthday card

3 Making a paper fan

a Fold the paper.

b Find photos.

c Draw a picture.

3 **Give it a go** Plan your instructions with a friend.

Choose what to create. → *Write step 1.* → *Draw a picture.*

I can shine!

4 Write your instructions together.

I can write instructions.

Our new hobbies

Step 1 Review

1 Look. Then ask and answer.

Tom		Luisa		Bartek	
🙂	☹	🙂	☹	🙂	☹
doing sport	using computers	playing chess	being outside	learning new things	doing crafts
helping people	taking photos	swapping cards	coding	juggling	finger knitting
learning an instrument	having parties	painting	acting	playing computer games	swapping cards

Does Luisa like acting?

No, she doesn't.

Does she like swapping cards?

Yes, she does!

2 Think of a friend. What activities does he / she like doing?

3 Think and write. Then compare with the class.

I'm good at... .	*I want to learn... .*

4 Tell a friend about a hobby you are good at.

1 What's the hobby?
2 Why do you like it?
3 How can your friend learn?

I'm good at coding. I like using computers. You can come to Coding Club and learn.

5 Watch and listen.

Step 2 Create

6 Choose a hobby you like.

7 Tell your group about your hobby. Invent a new hobby together.

I'm good at doing crafts.

I like doing sport.

I like swapping cards.

Let's make sports cards!

8 Create a sign for your new hobby.

Time to shine!

9 Present your new hobby to the class.

10 Choose a hobby you want to learn.

I can talk about learning something new.

Review 2 Our community

1 Listen. What are the books about?

2 Look. Ask and answer.

This book is about a… .

Does he like…?

3 Describe your friend.

He / She's… .

He / She likes… .

He / She's good at… .

4 Listen and read. Choose the best title.

The cute giant

The kind princess

This book is about a princess. She likes playing chess and painting pictures. But one day she wants to learn something new, so she goes on an adventure. She meets a scary giant and a cute dragon. The princess is kind, so she makes friends with the giant and the dragon. Now they like having parties at the castle!

It's a very interesting story!
Review by Clara

5 Read again. Then answer. *True* or *false*?

1 The princess doesn't like painting pictures.
2 The dragon is scary.
3 The princess is kind.
4 They don't like having parties.
5 Clara doesn't like the book.

MINI PROJECT

6 Create your own book cover.

This book is about... .
He / She's... .
He / She likes... .
One day... .

Time to shine!

7 What can you see in the courtyard? Complete your library record.

1	I can read, write and say book characters and activities.
2	I can describe book characters and say what my friends like.
3	I can agree and disagree.
4	I can ask friends what they're good at.

5 Let's save our animals!

Rise and Shine Library

- Talk about animals.
- Read about animals.
- Make and respond to suggestions.
- Write an animal fact file.
- Create an animal project.

I wonder... What birds can swim but can't fly?

1 tigers	2 penguins	3 monkeys	4 leopards	5 lions
6 snakes	7 pandas	8 zebras	9 rhinos	10 parrots

Lesson 1

What animals are there in your country?

What can you see?

1 5.01 Listen and find.

2 5.02 Listen and point. Then listen and repeat.

3 Watch and listen.

4 Look and say.

They're fast.

They're leopards!

Song

Look at the animals at the zoo,
Let's see what they can do.

Parrots can fly,
But can they sing?
Yes, they can,
But they can't swim.
Chorus

Tigers can run,
But can they walk?
Yes, they can,
But they can't talk!
Chorus

Penguins can swim,
But can they fly?
No, they can't,
I don't know why!
Chorus

Lesson 2

1 5.03 Read and sing.

2 5.05 Listen and answer.

3 Make sentences about the animals in the picture.

Grammar

Tigers **can** run.
They can't fly.
Can tigers run? Yes, **they can**.
Can they fly? No, **they can't**.

I can shine!

4 Ask and answer.

Can they run?
No, they can't.
Can they fly?
Yes, they can.
Are they parrots?
Yes, they are!

I can talk about animals.

Lesson 3

1 5.07 Listen, point and say.

1

spots

2

stripes

3

fur

4
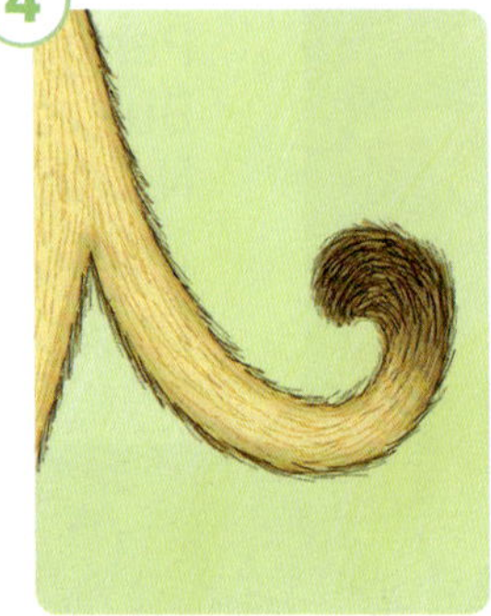
tail

5

feathers

6

wings

2 Look at the story. Find the animal parts from Activity 1.

3 5.08 Listen or watch. What are the special animals?

Rise and Shine **Library**

4 Read again. Then answer.

1 Choose words from the box to describe long-eared jerboas.

a long tail	small wings	feathers	fur
big ears	stripes	spots	

2 What can jerboas do?

I can shine!

5 Imagine you go to the zoo with Thomas. Act out.

I can read, understand and act out a story about animals.

Story value Appreciating all animals, big and small.

Lesson 4

1 Listen and number.

5.09

a

b

c

d

2 Listen and read. Then chant.

5.10

Grammar builder

They've got	fur.	
They haven't got	feathers.	
Have they got	spots?	Yes, they have.
	stripes?	No, they haven't.

Ask and answer about parrots.

3 Ask and answer.

They've got fur.

Yes, they have.

Have they got stripes?

They're... .

Structures *They've got / haven't got (fur). Have they got (spots)? Yes, they have. / No, they haven't.*

Lesson 5

1 Look. How can you learn about animals?

2 5.11 Listen and read. What do the children want to do?

3 5.12 Listen again and repeat.

Pronunciation

4 5.13 Listen and say.

Shall we learn about snakes with stripes and fish with spots? Yes!

I can shine!

5 Ask and answer. Choose an animal and how to learn about it.

Shall we learn about...?

Yes, that sounds great!

I can make and respond to suggestions.

Global Citizen
I appreciate animal habitats.

Lesson 6

1 Look. Which animals live in hot places?

2 5.14 Listen and read. Where do monkeys live?

Discover | Competitions | Games

Penguins live in the **ocean**. They've got wings and feathers, but they can't fly. Penguins swim with their wings! They swim very fast. It's very cold in the ocean and their feathers help them to stay warm. They like eating fish.

Lions live in **grassland**. It's very hot, so they sleep during the day. At night they catch their food. They've got strong legs, so they can run very fast.

Some snakes live in the **desert**. At night it's cold but during the day it's very hot. There isn't a lot of water, so snakes don't drink a lot. They eat eggs, birds, mice and other snakes!

Monkeys live in the **jungle** but some monkeys live in grassland and in cold habitats, too. They've got long arms and tails, and they can jump from tree to tree. It's hot in the jungle. There's a lot of fruit to eat. Monkeys love fruit!

3 Read again. Then answer. *True* or *false*?

1 Penguins live in the jungle.
2 Lions live in grassland.
3 Some snakes live in the desert.
4 Monkeys don't like fruit.

4 5.15 Listen. Which other animals live in grassland?

Lesson 7

1 5.17 Listen and read. What can tigers do?

Come and see the tigers!

These are tigers.
They live in the jungle.
They've got fur.
They've got stripes.
They can run, jump and swim.
They're in danger!
Let's protect the tigers!

Our writing workshop

2 5.18 **Ideas generator** Listen, read and match.

a

These are pandas. They've got a small tail and black and white fur. They can climb trees.

b

These are parrots. They live in the jungle. They've got beautiful feathers.

1

Laura

2

David

3 **Give it a go** Plan your fact file with a friend.

Choose an animal. → Where do they live? → What have they got? → What can they do?

I can shine!

4 Write your animal fact file together.

I can write an animal fact file.

Our animal project

Step 1 Review

1 Find the odd one out.

Snakes can't run.

1 lions snakes tigers
2 pandas parrots leopards
3 zebras rhinos penguins
4 rhinos monkeys pandas

2 Read and match.

Bird quiz

1 They've got wings. They can't fly but they can swim.

2 They've got feathers and wings. They can fly.

a

b

3 Ask and answer. Play *Guess the animal*!

Have they got...?

Can they...?

4 Tell a friend about your favourite animals.

1 Where do they live?
2 What have they got?
3 What can they do?
4 How can your friend learn more about them?

Pandas live in forests. They've got fur and can climb. You can read a book to learn about them.

5 Watch and listen.

Step 2 Create

6 Choose an animal for your project. Write.

They can / can't… .

They've got / haven't got… .

7 Tell your group about your animal. Decide what you want to do together.

Shall we…?

take pictures | *make a book* | *make a poster* | *look on the internet*

8 Create your project!

Time to shine!

9 Present your animal project to the class.

This is our poster. It's about rhinos.

They live in grassland but they're in danger.

10 What new facts do you know about animals?

They can run. They've got a tail.

Let's help the rhinos!

I can talk about animals.

6 Come on an adventure!

Rise and Shine Library

- Talk about what people are doing.
- Read about activities.
- Talk about the weather.
- Write a blog post.
- Create an adventure park.

I wonder...
What activities can you do when it's snowy?

1 having a picnic	2 building a den	3 fishing	4 cycling
5 skateboarding	6 reading a map	7 sailing	8 doing a nature trail
9 drawing	10 rock-climbing		

Lesson 1

What activities do you like? Why?

What can you see?

1 6.01 **Listen and find.**

2 6.02 **Listen and point. Then listen and repeat.**

3 **Watch and listen.**

4 **Look and say.**

I'm doing a nature trail.

You're Lena.

Song

They aren't in the library,
They aren't at school,
They're at the adventure park,
It's really cool!

Alicia isn't cycling,
She isn't playing with a ball,
She's learning something new,
She's rock-climbing up a wall.

Chorus

Daniel isn't fishing,
He isn't writing with his pens,
He's drawing a picture,
To share with all his friends.

Lena isn't sailing,
She isn't building a den,
She's doing a nature trail,
She's having an adventure again.

Chorus

Lesson 2

1 6.03 Read and sing.

2 6.05 Listen, find and say. Who is it?

3 Make sentences about the picture.

Grammar

He's fishing.	He isn't cycling.
She's rock-climbing.	She isn't sailing.

I can shine!

4 Act out the activities to your friends. Guess.

He isn't sailing.

He's fishing.

I can talk about what people are doing.

Lesson 3

1 6.07 Listen, point and say.

1

forest

2

lake

3

mountain

4

river

5

countryside

6

island

2 Look at the story. Find the places from Activity 1.

3 6.08 Listen or watch. What activities do the children do on the nature trail?

4 Read again. Then answer.

1. What can they see on the nature trail?
2. When it rains, what do they do?
3. What's Thomas reading?
4. Where's the library?

I can shine!

5 Imagine you're doing the nature trail with Thomas. Act out.

I can understand a story about activities.

Story value Having an adventure close to home.

Lesson 4

1 6.09 Listen and number.

a

b

c

d

2 6.10 Listen and read. Then chant.

Ask and answer about the characters.

Grammar builder

	What's he doing?	*He's*	*drawing.*
Is he	*skateboarding?*	*Yes, he is.*	
Is she	*cycling?*	*No, she isn't.*	

3 Ask and answer.

Is she building a den?

No, she isn't.

What's she doing?

She's sailing.

Structures *What's he doing? He's (skateboarding). Is she (cycling)? Yes, she is. / No, she isn't.*

Lesson 5

1 Look. What weather can you see?

2 6.11 Listen and read. What activity do they want to do?

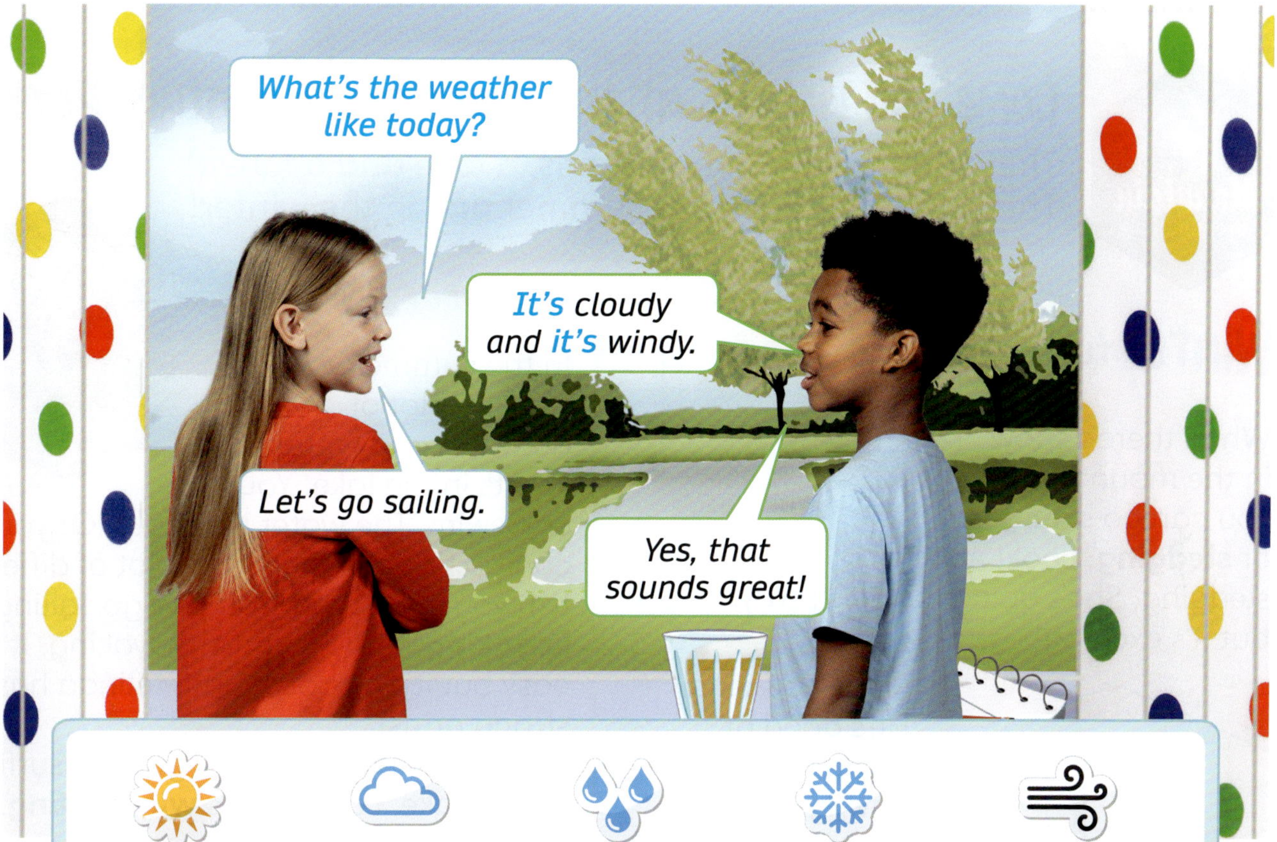

sunny | cloudy | rainy | snowy | windy

3 6.12 Listen again and repeat.

Pronunciation

4 6.13 Listen and say.

Snowy weather, snowy weather,
Let's play in the snow together!

I can shine!

5 Ask and answer. Find out what the weather's like.

What's the weather like?

It's... .

Let's... .

I can talk about the weather.

Lesson 6

1 Look. Where can you do the activities?

2 6.14 Listen and read. What's Mountain Adventure Park?

Mountain Adventure Park

Come and visit us at the Mountain Adventure Park.

There are beautiful mountains, a lake and a forest! There's a lot to do in the summer and in the winter!

Winter fun!

When there's snow in the mountains you can go **skiing** or **sledging**. Look! Alina's sledging. She's going fast! It's scary, but it's exciting!

Roman's skiing. He's good at skiing, and he's having fun! If you can't ski, don't worry! You can have lessons.

Fun Fact! Some people can ski very fast – 200 km per hour!

Summer fun!

In the summer you can do a lot of activities and water sports in the lake. You can swim. The water isn't cold. Or you can go fishing. There are a lot of different fish you can catch. You can go sailing or **kayaking**, too. Melinda's kayaking. It isn't easy but it's a cool sport! Melinda has got strong arms!
When it's windy, you can go windsurfing on the lake. Look, Ewa's **windsurfing**. She's very happy!

If you don't like water sports, you can go rock-climbing or do nature trails in the forest. Or you can go cycling or walking.

The Mountain Adventure Park is a fantastic place for a holiday!

3 Read again. Then answer.

1 Where can you go sledging?
2 Who likes skiing?
3 What activities can you do on the lake?
4 What activity can you do when it's windy?

4 6.15 Listen. What does Helga do in the summer?

Lesson 7

1 6.17 Listen and read. What activity is Mia doing?

Woodfield Primary School Home About Blog

Home > Blog > School Trip

My school trip to the countryside

by Mia, class 3B

This is me with my friends. We're on a school trip in the countryside. We're having fun! There's a big forest with nature trails. There's a river, too. I'm building a den in the forest.
Paolo's doing a nature trail. Sam's fishing in the river and Rachel's drawing a picture of some flowers.

Our writing workshop

2 6.18 **Ideas generator** Listen, read and complete.

1 We're on a school trip in the.... Adam's.... .

2 We're on a school trip in the… . I'm… .

3 **Give it a go** Plan your blog post with a friend.

Where's your school trip?

What are you doing?

What's your friend doing?

I can shine!

4 Write your blog post together.

I can write a blog post.

Our adventure parks

Step 1 Review

1 Write the words.

sailing cycling fishing sledging windsurfing having a picnic
doing a nature trail building a den skiing

forest	lake	mountains

2 Look. Ask and answer.

What's the boy doing?

3 Look at the pictures in Activity 2. Talk about the weather.

What's the weather like?

It's... .

4 Tell a friend about activities you do.

1 What activities do you do in the summer?
2 What activities do you do in the winter?
3 What activities do you do all year?

In the summer I like having a picnic. I like drawing in the winter. I like cycling all year.

5 Watch and listen.

Step 2 Create

6 Choose a place for your adventure park.

7 Tell your group about your adventure park. Decide some summer and winter activities together.

What's the weather like?

It's sunny in the summer.

Let's have fishing at the lake in our adventure park.

Yes, that sounds great.

8 Create your adventure park advert.

Time to shine!

9 Present your advert to the class.

10 Choose an adventure park to visit.

I can talk about an adventure park.

Review 3 Our world

1 Listen. What animals are in the grassland?

2 Look. Ask and answer.

Have they got…? — stripes feathers fur spots legs tails wings

Can they…? — climb run jump swim walk fly

3 What animals live in these places?

jungles oceans deserts grassland

4 Listen and read. Where's Jamie?

POSTCARD

Dear Granny,
We're on holiday in the jungle. It's winter but it's hot and rainy. There are leopards, parrots and snakes here! It's amazing! I'm doing a nature trail in the jungle with Dad. Mum's drawing pictures of the animals and Ben's building a den. There's a big lake in the jungle but Theo isn't fishing. He's kayaking! We're all having fun!
See you soon!
Jamie

3 New Road
Rivertown

5 Read again. Then answer.

1 What's the weather like?
2 What animals are there?
3 What's Jamie's mum doing?
4 Is Theo fishing?

MINI PROJECT

6 Write your own holiday postcard.

POSTCARD

Dear... .
I'm on holiday in... .
There's / There are... .
I'm... .
My friend's... .
See you soon!

Time to shine!

7 What can you see in the courtyard? Complete your library record.

1	I can read, write and say animals and outdoor activities.
2	I can say what animals can do and what friends are doing.
3	I can make and respond to suggestions.
4	I can ask and answer about the weather.

Goodbye from The Rise and Shine Library

What can you see?

1 7.01 Listen or watch. Does Biscuit like the courtyard?

2 7.02 Listen again. Which words from the box do you hear?

doctor	lions	poster	bus stop
party	monster	rock-climbing	

Song

Goodbye! Goodbye!
It's time to say,
Have a happy holiday!
It's summer time,
There's no more school!
Have a good summer,
See you soon!

Goodbye Daniel and Rafa,
Goodbye Lena and Alicia,
Goodbye Thomas and Biscuit too!
Have a good summer,
See you soon!

Chorus

Test your progress with English Benchmark Young Learners

3 Read and sing.

4 Ask and answer.

Who's your favourite character in Rise and Shine? Why?

Which is your favourite unit? Why?

I can shine!

5 Choose something new to put in the courtyard. Write and say.

I want to put my favourite book in the courtyard.

World Teachers' Day

What can you see?

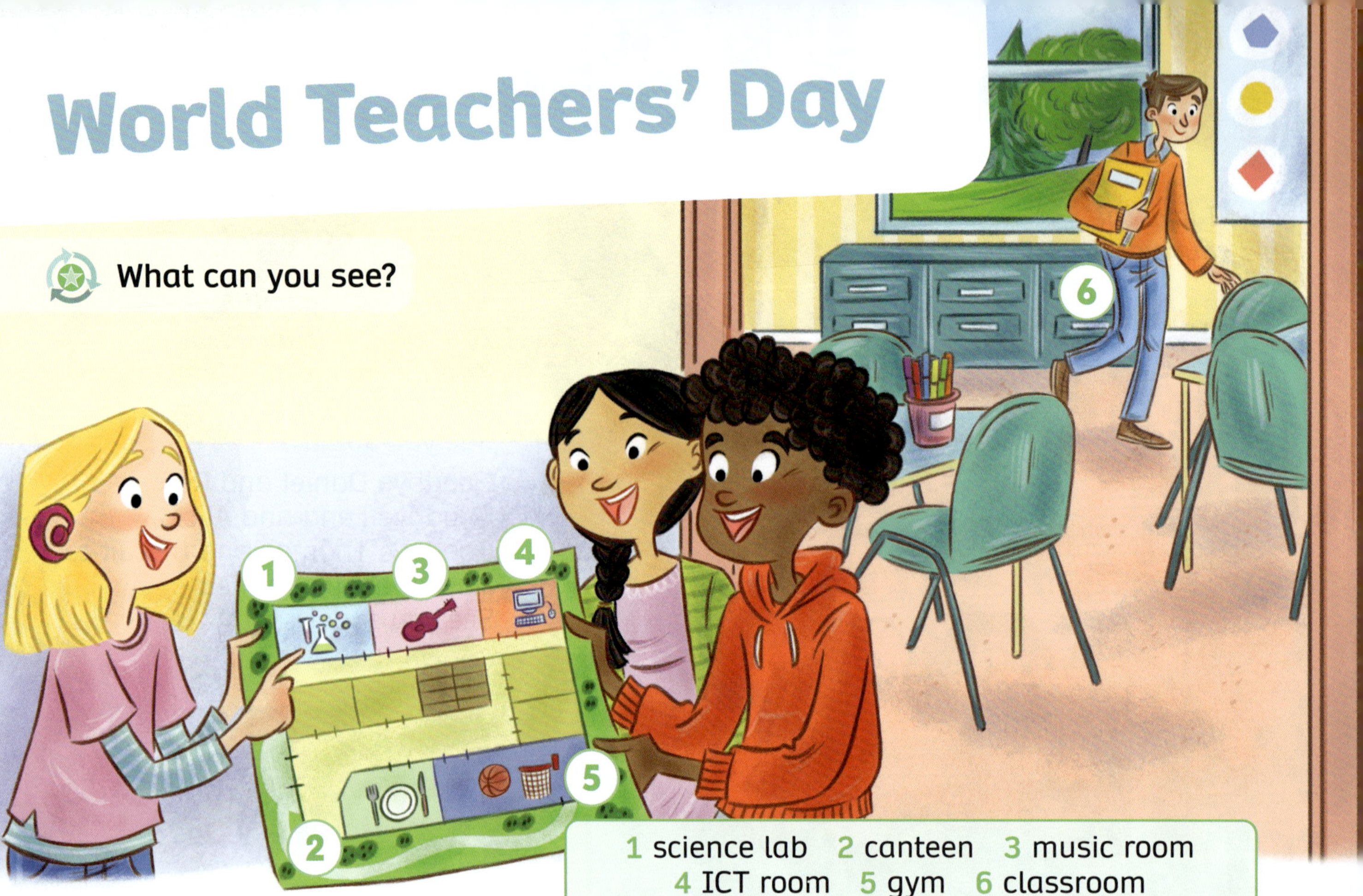

1 science lab 2 canteen 3 music room
4 ICT room 5 gym 6 classroom

1 8.01 Listen and find.

2 8.02 Listen and point. Then listen and repeat.

3 8.03 Listen, read and point to the map. Then say.

Hurray for our teachers!
They're kind and they help us.
Teachers in the science lab and the music room.
Hurray for our teachers!
They're kind and they help us.
Teachers in the gym and the ICT room, too.
All the teachers help me and you!

Who's your favourite teacher?

4 Make a card for your favourite teacher.

World Kindness Day

What can you see?

1 help someone 2 smile
3 give someone a gift 4 care about someone
5 say thank you 6 talk to a friend

1 8.05 Listen and find.

2 8.06 Listen and point. Then listen and repeat.

3 8.07 Listen and read. Then say and act out.

It's World Kindness Day!
Let's be kind,
Let's all play.
Talk to a friend, smile, too.
Help someone and say thank you!

4 Make a class kindness book.

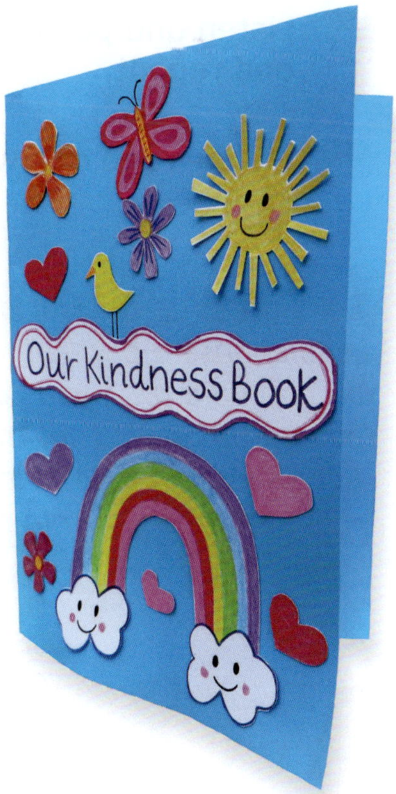

World Book Day

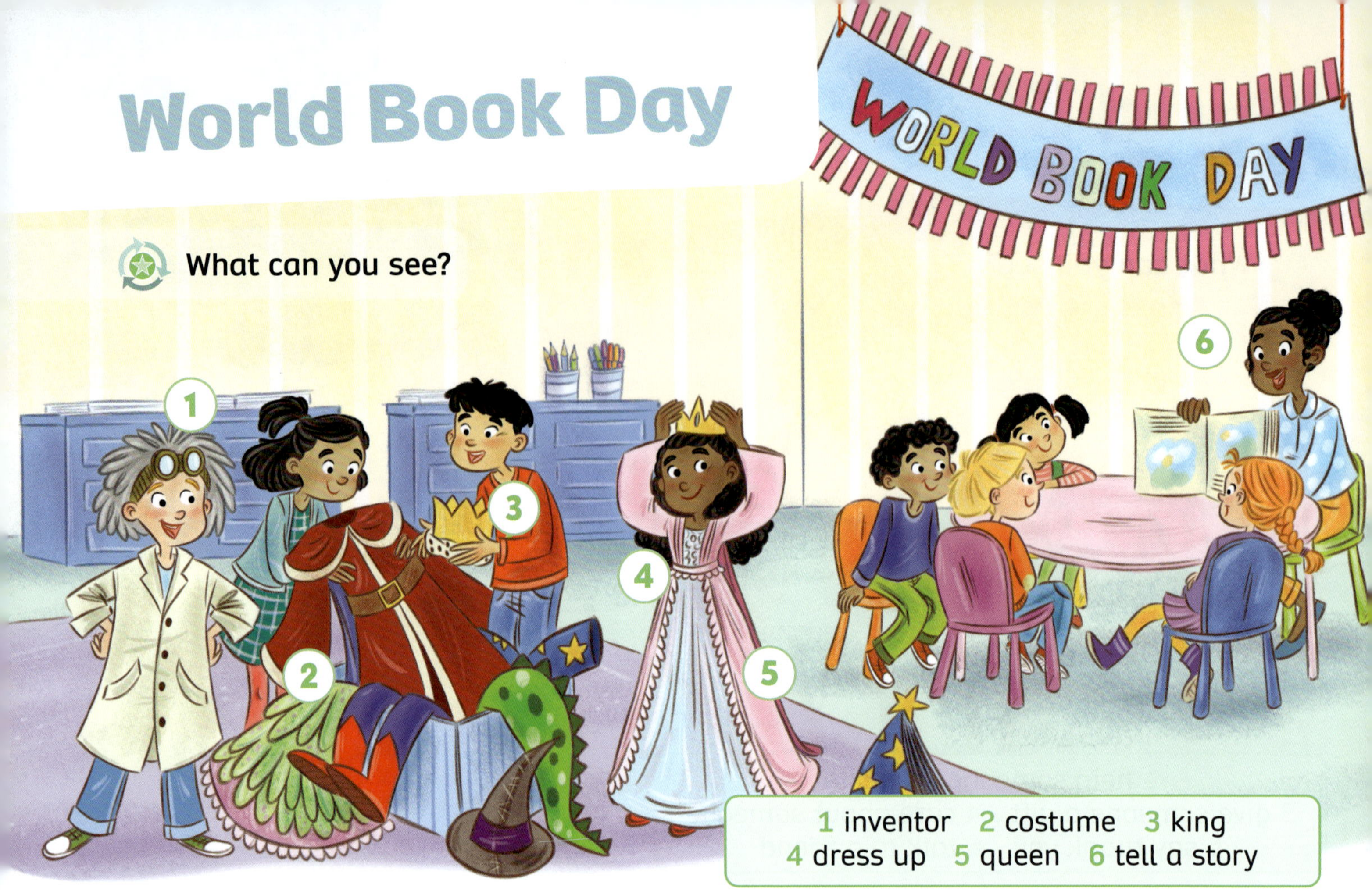

What can you see?

1 inventor 2 costume 3 king
4 dress up 5 queen 6 tell a story

1 8.09 Listen and find.

2 8.10 Listen and point. Then listen and repeat.

3 8.11 Listen, read and write. Then say.

Let's dress up for World Book Day!
Let's choose a c… – hip-hip-hurray!
You can be a q… , you can be a k… ,
You can be an i… that makes things!
Let's dress up for World Book Day!
Let's tell stories – hip-hip-hurray!

4 Create a cover for your favourite story.

What do you want to dress up as for World Book Day?

World Environment Day

What can you see?

1 8.13 Listen and find.

2 8.14 Listen and point. Then listen and repeat.

3 8.15 Listen, read and write. Then say and act out!

We can help the planet!
We can save w… in the shower.
We can grow v… .
Children power!
We can help the planet!
We can walk to s… .
We can turn off l… .
Children are cool!

4 Make a 'save the planet' wreath.

1 Listen and read. Why's Sara sad?

9.01

2 How does Sara feel at the end of the story? Why?

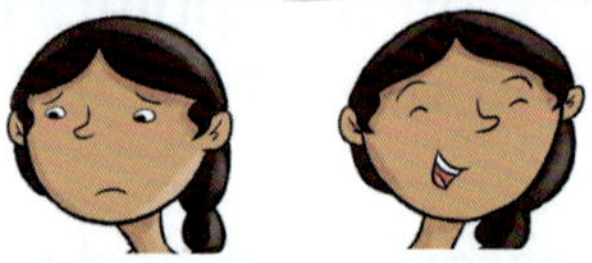

3 What can you say when a friend is sad?

- Are you OK?
- You can play with us.
- ...
- ...

Useful language

Let's go outside.
Let's play.
Let's draw.

Time to shine!

4 Imagine and act out.

Your friend doesn't want to go to the park with you.

Are you OK?

I don't want to go to the park.

The park's fun!

Reflect How do you know when a friend is sad?

1 9.02 Listen and read. What's the problem in the park?

2 Who cleans up the park?

3 What can you do to help in your park?

- Don't drop things.
- Help other people.
- …
- …

Useful language

We can help you.
We can clean up the park together.
Shall we plant some trees?

Time to shine!

4 Imagine and act out.

You want to clean up the playground with your friends.

Shall we clean up the playground?

Sure. I can help you.

Reflect When you are at the park, what can you see, hear and smell?

1 9.03 Listen and read. Who's good at listening?

2 How does Jack feel at the end of the story? Why?

3 How can we be good at listening?

- Look at the person when they speak.
- Don't speak when someone is speaking.
- …
- …

Useful language

Be quiet, please.
Please listen.

Time to shine!

4 Imagine and act out.

Your friend is reading instructions to you. What do you do?

Please listen.

Reflect Is it easy or difficult to listen?

1 9.04 Listen and read. What does Kiera want to learn?

2 How does Kiera learn something new?

3 How can you learn something new?

- Ask a friend.
- Practise.
- ...
- ...

Useful language

I want to learn... .
Can you teach me?
I'm good at... .

Time to shine!

4 Imagine and act out.

You want to learn something new.

I want to learn the guitar.

Who can help you?

My sister, Nadia.

Reflect When something is difficult, don't give up. Take a break and try again.

Future skills 5 Making decisions

1 9.05 Listen and read. Why are Zain and Kiera angry?

2 How does everyone feel at the end of the story? Why?

3 What can you say when you and your friend have different ideas?

- I don't like arguments.
- Shall we... ?
- ...
- ...

Useful language

I've got an idea.
Let's make a list.
Let's do something different.

Time to shine!

4 Imagine and act out.

Your friend wants to play football. You want to stay inside and play computer games.

Shall we play football?

I don't want to. Let's do something different.

Reflect What do you like doing with your friends?

1 9.06 Listen and read. What problem does Kiera have?

2 How does Kiera solve the problem?

3 What can you do if something is difficult?

- Draw or write different ideas.
- Ask for help.
- …
- …

Useful language

Can you help me?
Let's use… .
Good idea!

Time to shine!

4 Imagine and act out.

You can't do your homework. What do you do?

I can't do my ICT homework. Can you help?

Sure! I love computers. What's the problem?

Reflect Sometimes there are different ways to solve a problem.

1 Read and complete.

REMEMBER!

What time **do** you wake up?

got wake do What

[1]... subjects have you got on Monday?

What time [3]... you wake up?

I 've [2]... Maths, English and Art.

I [4]... up at seven o'clock.

2 Listen and answer for Helen. *True* or *false?*

10.01

1 I wake up at six o'clock.

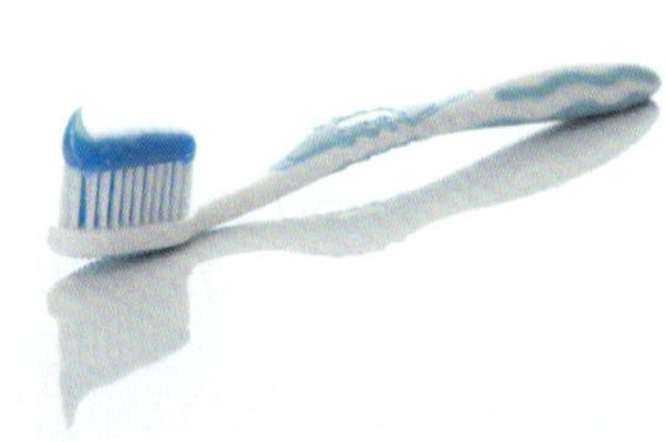

2 I brush my teeth.

3 I go to work by car.

4 I go to bed at nine o'clock.

3 Write about your weekend.

I wake up at... .

I've got... on Saturday.

I... on Sunday.

I go to bed at... .

Grammar

What subjects **have you got** on Monday?
I've got Maths and Science.
What activities **have you got** on Saturday?
I've got drama club.

4 Ask and answer.

What time do you wake up?

I wake up at eight o'clock.

What activities have you got at the weekend?

I've got a piano lesson on Saturday. I like Music.

1 Read and complete.

there any are is isn't

REMEMBER!

There are some shops.
There aren't any cars.

Is there a bookshop?

Is ²… a supermarket?

Are there ⁴… shops?

Yes, there ¹….

No, there ³….

Yes, there ⁵….

2 10.02 Listen and choose. What's in the school?

1

2

3

4

3 Imagine a new school. Write.

There's a… .
There isn't a… .
There are some… .
There aren't any… .

Grammar

Is there a café?
Yes, there is. / No, there isn't.
Are there any classrooms?
Yes, there are. / No, there aren't.

4 Ask and answer.

Is there a gym?

No, there isn't, but there's a playground.

Are there any tablets?

Yes, there are.

1 Read and complete.

> **REMEMBER!**
> Is she brave?
> Are they brave?

aren't They're Are about are they

What's the film about?

The film is [1]... a brother and a sister. [2]... astronauts.

[3]... they scary?

No, they [4]... .

Are [5]... brave?

Yes, they [6]... .

2 10.03 Listen and answer. *True* or *false?*

1 The film is about tigers.
2 The tigers are scary.
3 The girl isn't a princess.
4 She's brave.
5 The tigers aren't strong.
6 The film is interesting.

3 Write about your favourite film.

The film is about... .
He's / She's... .
He / She isn't... .
They're... .
They aren't... .
I think the film is... .

> **Grammar**
> The film is about tigers and a princess.
> Are the tigers scary?
> Yes, they are. / No, they aren't.
> Is the princess strong?
> Yes, she is. / No, she isn't.

4 Ask and answer.

What's your favourite film about?

It's about a family in the jungle.

Are the family brave?

Yes, they are.

Grammar 4

1 Read and complete.

REMEMBER!
She likes playing computer games.

does Does doesn't like likes

She [1]… acting.

Yes, she [3]….

No, he [5]….

Does she [2]… painting?

[4]… he like playing chess?

2 10.04 Listen and match.

1 Bibi 2 Sam 3 Jen 4 Tweedy

a

b

c

d

3 Write about someone in your family.

This is… .

He/She likes… .

He/She doesn't like… .

He's/She's good at… .

Grammar

My grandad likes being outside.
Does he like doing sport?
Yes he does. / No, he doesn't.

4 Ask and answer.

This is my aunt.

Does she like swapping cards?

No, she doesn't. She likes reading.

REMEMBER!

Can tigers run?
Yes, they can.

1 Read and complete.

got can haven't can't have

Zebras ¹… run.

Can snakes talk?

Have leopards ⁴… spots?

Parrots ²… got fur.

No, they ³….

Yes, they ⁵….

2 Listen and answer. *True* or *false?*

10.05

1 They've got long hair.
2 They've got blue eyes.
3 They can't swim.
4 They can juggle.
5 They can't paint.
6 They've got a dog.

3 Write about two friends.

These are my… .
They've got… .
They haven't got… .
They can… .

Grammar

Have your friends got brown eyes?
Yes, they have. / No, they haven't.
Can they play an instrument?
Yes, they can. / No, they can't.

4 Ask and answer.

My friends are Harry and Daniel.

Have they got short hair?

Yes, they have.

Can they code?

Yes, they can.

REMEMBER!

She's building a den.

1 Read and complete.

drawing What's Is isn't she

¹... he doing?

³... she cycling?

Is she sailing?

He's ²....

Yes, ⁴... is.

No, she ⁵....

2 10.06 Listen and match.

1 The police officer is...
2 The shop assistant is...
3 The waiter is...
4 Laura's...

a reading a book.
b talking to the man.
c drawing a picture.
d taking a photo.

3 Imagine you are in a town square. Write.

The police officer is... .

The waiter is... .

The shop assistant is... .

The bus driver is... .

My friend is... .

Grammar

What's he doing? He's painting.

Is she cycling? Yes, she is.

Is he reading a book?

No, he isn't. He's reading a map.

4 Ask and answer.

Is the bus driver driving the bus?

No, she isn't.

What's the bus driver doing?

She's eating a sandwich at the café.

The Rise and Shine Library Trail

Contents

Scope and sequence

	Vocabulary	Grammar	Global Citizenship	Project
Welcome to The Rise and Shine Library	**Numbers 20–50; places in a library:** courtyard, gallery, information desk, multimedia room, reading corner, study area **Library objects:** beanbag, computer, poster, television	The library has / hasn't got (a gallery). Has the library got (computers)? Yes, it has. / No, it hasn't. What time is it? It's (one o'clock / half past one).	**Appreciating community spaces** An activity flyer	A library record
1 All about school!	**School subjects:** Art, Drama, English, Geography, History, ICT, Maths, Music, PE, Science **Routine actions:** brush my teeth, go to bed, go to school, have breakfast, have a shower, wake up	What have you got (on Monday)? I've got (Art) on Monday. What time do you (wake up)? I wake up at half past six. How do you go to school? I go to school by (bus).	**Different school days:** classroom, homework, playground, timetable A diary entry	A photo diary
2 Explore our town! **Review 1** All about us	**Places in town:** bus stop, café, cinema, hospital, pharmacy, police station, shop, sports centre, supermarket, town square **Jobs:** bus driver, doctor, librarian, police officer, shop assistant, waiter	There are some (shops). There aren't any (schools). Is there a (librarian)? Yes, there is. / No, there isn't. Are there any (police officers)? Yes, there are. / No, there aren't. Where do you live? I live on (Park Street).	**Different towns:** bench, community, fountain, friendly A leaflet	A town map
3 Let's tell stories!	**Book characters:** astronaut, dragon, giant, monster, pirate, prince, princess, spy, storyteller, superhero **Adjectives:** brave, clever, cute, kind, scary, strong	The book is about (a giant). Is she (happy)? Yes, she is. No, she isn't. Are they (clever)? Yes, they are. / No, they aren't. I think... Oh, I do. / So do I!	**Storytelling:** beautiful, exciting, fun, interesting A book review	A story character
4 Party at the library! **Review 2** Our community	**Hobbies:** acting, coding, having a party, juggling, learning an instrument, painting, playing chess, playing computer games, swapping cards, taking photos **Activities:** being outside, doing crafts, doing sport, helping people, learning something new, using computers	She likes (taking photos). He doesn't like (playing chess). Does he / she like doing sport? Yes, he / she does. / No, he / she doesn't. Are you good at coding? Yes, I am. / No, I'm not. I want to learn.	**Hobbies and crafts:** cut, fold, knit, stick Instructions	A new hobby
5 Let's save our animals!	**Animals:** lions, leopards, monkeys, pandas, parrots, penguins, rhinos, snakes, tigers, zebras **Animal parts:** feathers, fur, spots, stripes, tail, wings	(Tigers) can / can't (run). Can they (fly)? Yes, they can. / No, they can't. They've got / haven't got (fur). Have they got (spots)? Yes, they have. / No, they haven't. Shall we (watch a film)? Yes, that sounds great. / I'm not sure.	**Animal habitats:** desert, grassland, jungle, ocean An animal fact file	An animal project
6 Come on an adventure! **Review 3** Our world	**Outdoor activities:** building a den, cycling, doing a nature trail, drawing, fishing, having a picnic, reading a map, rock-climbing, sailing, skateboarding **Places in nature:** countryside, forest, island, lake, mountain, river	He's / She's (fishing). He / She isn't (cycling). What's he / she doing? He / She's (skateboarding). Is he / she (cycling)? Yes, he / she is. / No, he / she isn't. What's the weather like today? It's (windy).	**Outdoor activities:** kayaking, skiing, sledging, windsurfing A blog post	An adventure park advert

Goodbye	**Have a good summer! See you soon!**
Celebrations	**World Teachers' Day, World Kindness Day, World Book Day, World Environment Day**
Future skills	**Encouraging others, Community spaces, Listening, Learning to learn, Making decisions, Problem solving**

Pronunciation	
Unit 1 /ɔɪ/, /ɔː/	**Unit 4** /ɜː/, /ɪŋ/
Unit 2 /eə/, /ɑː/	**Unit 5** /s/, /ʃ/
Unit 3 /b/, /v/	**Unit 6** /ə/, /əʊ/

My Progress Chart

	Welcome	Unit 1	Unit 2	Unit 3	Unit 4	Unit 5	Unit 6
Listening	I can understand my phrases and sentences in dialogues.	I can understand short, simple questions on familiar topics.		I can understand important information in short conversations.		I can identify people and things from short descriptions.	
Reading	I can read short stories and notice information.	I can read and understand simple descriptions.		I can understand the important ideas in short texts.		I can read and understand some details in short texts.	
Speaking	I can talk about myself and my world.	I can ask and answer questions about my community.		I can describe and give information about the world around me.		I can have a short conversation about my world.	
Writing	I can write my words and phrases.	I can write a sentence and spell my words.		I can write a simple sentence to give information.		I can write simple sentences about the world around me.	

Welcome to The Rise and Shine Library

1 information desk 2 multimedia room 3 gallery
4 reading corner 5 courtyard 6 study area

Lesson 1

What can you see?

1 0.04 **Listen and find.**

2 0.05 **Listen and point. Then listen and repeat.**

3 **Look and say.**

Thomas has got brown hair.

There's a photo on the information desk.

What time do you have breakfast in the morning?
What places are there in your town?
This animal has got spots. It can run very fast. What is it?
Does your friend like being outside?
What's your favourite book about?

Pearson Education Limited
KAO Two
KAO Park
Hockham Way
Harlow, Essex
CM17 9SR
England
and Associated Companies throughout the world.

pearsonenglish.com

First published 2021
Seventh impression 2024

ISBN: 978-1-292-36930-3

Set in Daytona Pro Primary

Printed in Slovakia by Neografia

Acknowledgements
The publisher would like to thank the following for their kind permission to
reproduce their photographs:

(Key: b-bottom c-centre l-left r-right t-top)

123RF.com: Anna Grigorjeva 14, belchonock 89, Craig Robinson 71, Richard Thomas 21, Wavebreak Media Ltd 14; **Alamy Stock Photo:** Encore 15, 19, Geopix 88, graficart.net 24, Heather Drake 26, imageBROKER 58, IndiaPicture 38, Kirk Fisher 93, NordicImages 15, robertharding 27, Shotshop GmbH 54, Stephen French 89, SuperStock 38, Taina Sohlman 15, View Stock 16, Wayne Hutchison 36, Westend61 GmbH 49, Xinhua 38; **Getty Images:** 81a/Photolibrary 8, ALEAIMAGE 88, andresr 36, Andrew Bret Wallis 60, Ariel Skelley 24, artisteer 42, baona 89, Bruno Guerreiro 62, Camille Tokerud 71, creativesunday2016 5, dcdebs 61, Dennis Glosik/500px 62, elenaleonova 19, Fuse 54, Gallo Images 58, gbh007 27, GlobalStock 46, jacobeukman 58, jez_bennett 60, JGI/Jamie Grill 61, Johner Images 70, JohnnyGreig 17, Jose Luis Pelaez Inc 27, 91, kali9 27, katoosha 38, Keren Su 62, Lane Oatey/Blue Jean Images 16, Londolozi Images/Mint Images 63, Maica 91, Maskot 26, 89, Miguel Sanz 63, Mirrorimage-NL 43, monkeybusinessimages 89, NickyBlade 21, Nirad 77, orangelinemedia 91, Patrik Giardino 46, PeopleImages 90, photoquest7 24, Pitipat Usanakornkul/EyeEm 36, princessdlaf 8, Richard Drury 71, Skip Brown 70, SolStock 46, Stephan Jaggy/500px 62, Stockbyte 27, 92, Tim Hall 71, unclepodger 11, ValuaVitaly 27, viafilms 19, webguzs 60, Westend61 68, 68, ziggy_mars 46, Zoran Kolundzija 61; **Pearson Education Ltd:** Jon Barlow 9, 15, 19, 25, 29, 36, 37, 41, 47, 49, 51, 59, 63, 69, 73, 88, 89, 90, 91, 92, 93, Studio 8 91, Terry Leung 49, Trevor Clifford 8; **Shutterstock.com:** 8, 24, Alexandr Shevchenko 88, BCFC 88, Becky Wass 70, Bobkeenan Photography 64, cowardlion 16, 16, doomu 7, Dragon Images 48, Edge Digital Imaging 19, Elena Elisseeva 15, esthermm 14, FamVeld 68, Fotofermer 77, fotosaga 49, Hung Chung Chih 58, inaina 16, Jack N. Mohr 65, Jeanette Virginia Goh 48, John Abbate 32, Paul Vinten 60, Petr Bonek 70, RedKoala 69, Roman Gorielov 32, Spotmatik Ltd 68, Syda Productions 26, Tatyano O 48, Toms Auzins 26, Tramont_ana 76, travellifestyle 88, VaLiza 26

Cover Images: *Front*: **123RF.com:** Gabriel Murad; **Alamy Stock Photo:** View Stock

All other images © Pearson Education

Illustrated by BluBlu Studios (main character artwork); Emma Allen /Sylvie Poggio: pp. 6, 12, 22, 34, 44, 56, 66; Valentina Bandera /Sylvie Poggio: pp. 9, 28, 40, 72;Ruth Bennett /The Bright Agency pp: 82-87; Lyn Dylan /Sylvie Poggio: pp. 15 (Ex 1), 25 (Ex 1), 37 (Ex 1), 47 (Ex 1), 59 (Ex 1); Jen Naalchigar /The Bright Agency: pp. 61; Elisa Rocchi /Beehive Illustration: pp. 78-81; Simona Rossi /Sylvie Poggio: pp. 30, 52, 74; Ana Sebastian /The Bright Agency: pp. 15, 25, 37, 47, 59, 69 pronunciation; Skylar White /The Bright Agency: pp. 8, 27, 39.

https://www.un.org/sustainabledevelopment/
The content of this publication has not been approved by the United Nations and does not reflect the views of the United Nations or its officials or Member States.